ASK ISAAC ASIMOV ?

What is a shooting star?

Heinemann

First published in Great Britain by Heinemann Library
an imprint of Heinemann Publishers (Oxford) Ltd
Halley Court, Jordan Hill, Oxford OX2 8EJ

OXFORD LONDON EDINBURGH MADRID
ATHENS BOLOGNA PARIS MELBOURNE
SYDNEY AUCKLAND SINGAPORE TOKYO
IBADAN NAIROBI HARARE GABORONE
PORTSMOUTH NH (USA)

98 97 96 95 94

10 9 8 7 6 5 4 3 2 1

British Library Cataloguing in Publication Data is available from the British Library on request.

ISBN 0 431 07650 2

Cover designed and pages typeset by Philip Parkhouse
Printed in China

Picture Credits
pp. 2-3, Paul Dimare; pp. 4-5, Rick Karpinski/DeWalt and Associates; pp. 6-7, © Frank Zullo; pp. 8-9, Paul Dimare; pp. 10-11, John Sanford/Science Photo Library; pp. 10-11 (border), courtesy of NASA; pp. 12-13, © Gareth Stevens, Inc.; p. 14 (inset), © Edward J. Olsen; pp. 14-15, Mark Maxwell; pp. 16-17, Mary Evans Picture Library; pp. 18-19, Frank Zullo, © 1986; p. 20, Mark Mille/DeWalt and Associates; p. 21, © Gareth Stevens, Inc.; pp. 22-24, Rick Karpinski/DeWalt and Associates

Cover photo © Science Photo Library/David McLean
Back cover photograph © Sygma/D. Kirkland

Series editor: Elizabeth Kaplan
Editor: Patricia Lantier-Sampon
Series designer: Sabine Huschke
Picture researcher: Daniel Helminak
Picture research assistant: Diane Laska
Consulting editor: Matthew Groshek

Contents

Words that appear in the glossary are printed in **bold** the first time
they occur in the text.

A world of questions

Our world is full of strange and beautiful things. The night sky glimmers with **stars**. Lightning flashes from dark clouds during a thunderstorm. Sometimes we have questions about the things we see. Asking questions helps us to appreciate the wonders of the universe.

For instance, have you ever seen a shooting star? Look at the sky on a dark, clear night and you may see a star moving across the sky. This is a shooting star. It may also be called a 'falling star'. But is it really a star? Does it really fall? Let's find out.

4

What does a shooting star look like?

A shooting star is not just a point of light as other stars are. A shooting star looks like a streak of light, as shown on the left. It flashes across the sky and then disappears. Towards the end it may get brighter. In rare cases it can explode. Usually it just fades after a second or two.

Once the shooting star is gone, all the ordinary stars remain in the sky. No matter how many shooting stars you see, the ordinary stars do not disappear.

What is a shooting star?

A shooting star is not a real star. It is a piece of rock zooming through the Earth's **atmosphere**. The rock's motion through the air heats it so much it becomes white-hot. This is why it makes a glowing streak. Scientists call such a rock a **meteor**.

Most meteors are about the size of a piece of dust. They burn up completely in the air above the Earth. A few meteors are so large they don't burn up and what is left hits the ground. A meteor that hits the ground is called a **meteorite**.

How is a crater made?

When a really big meteorite crashes into the Earth, it gouges out a hole called a **crater**. In Arizona, USA, there is a crater 1.2 kilometres across and 180 metres deep.

10

We do not find many craters on Earth. Most of the craters have been overgrown with plants or worn away by wind and rain. Craters are common, however, on the Moon and on Mercury. On these planets without wind, rain or life, craters can last for billions of years.

11

How to spot a meteorite

People sometimes find meteorites after they
have fallen. Most meteorites are made of
rock. These meteorites, including the one
above, look similar to other rocks on Earth.
A meteorite is hard to identify unless you
actually see one fall or hear it hit the
ground. A few meteorites are made mainly
of metals, such as **iron** and **nickel**. These
meteorites, including the ones on the right,
are magnetic and look different from most
rocks on Earth.

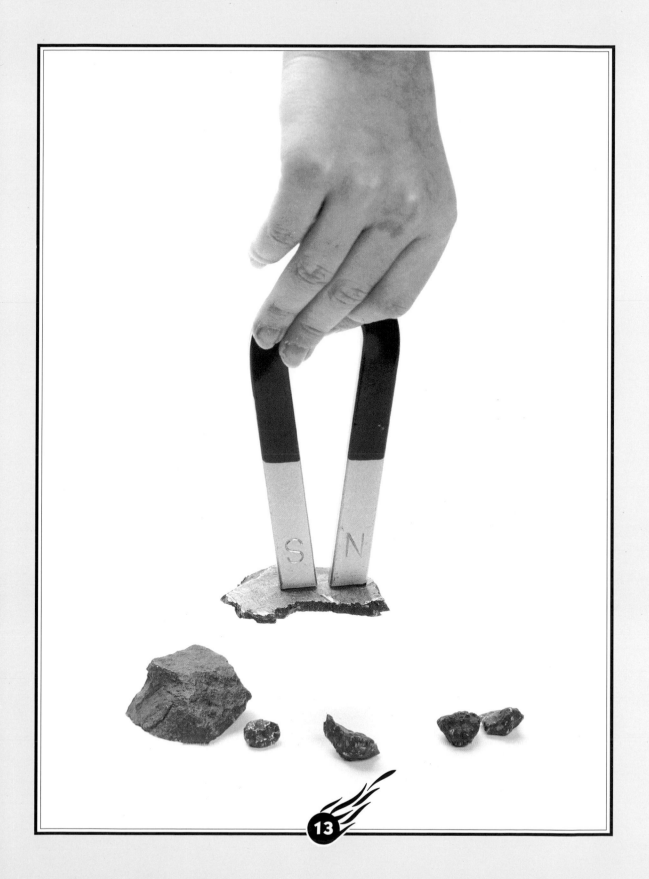

Cosmic explosion

Some meteors are rocks broken off from the Moon, other planets or **heavenly bodies**. For example, if a large object collides with a planet, huge pieces of rock are blasted away from the planet's surface. The rocks fly into space. They may orbit the Sun for millions of years. They may swing close to Earth and eventually crash into our planet. Scientists have found meteorites in Antarctica which came from the Moon and some which may have come from Mars.

What is a meteor shower?

Some meteors come from **comets**. Comets are bits of rock and dust frozen in a ball of ice. If a comet skims near the Sun, the Sun's heat melts the comet and a cloud of dust and rock is all that remains. Earth sometimes passes through these dusty clouds. The dust enters the Earth's atmosphere and forms a shower of meteors. This picture shows a spectacular **meteor shower** in 1870 when the Earth passed through a cloud of dust. Meteors swarmed in the night sky like snowflakes.

Watch the stars and see how they fall

On any given night, shooting stars streak across the sky. However, certain times of the year are better for watching shooting stars than others. Some calendars show times when meteor showers will occur.

During an average meteor shower, you can see as many as 60 shooting stars in an hour! Choose a clear, moonless night when there is a meteor shower, and go to a place away from street lights to enjoy the show.

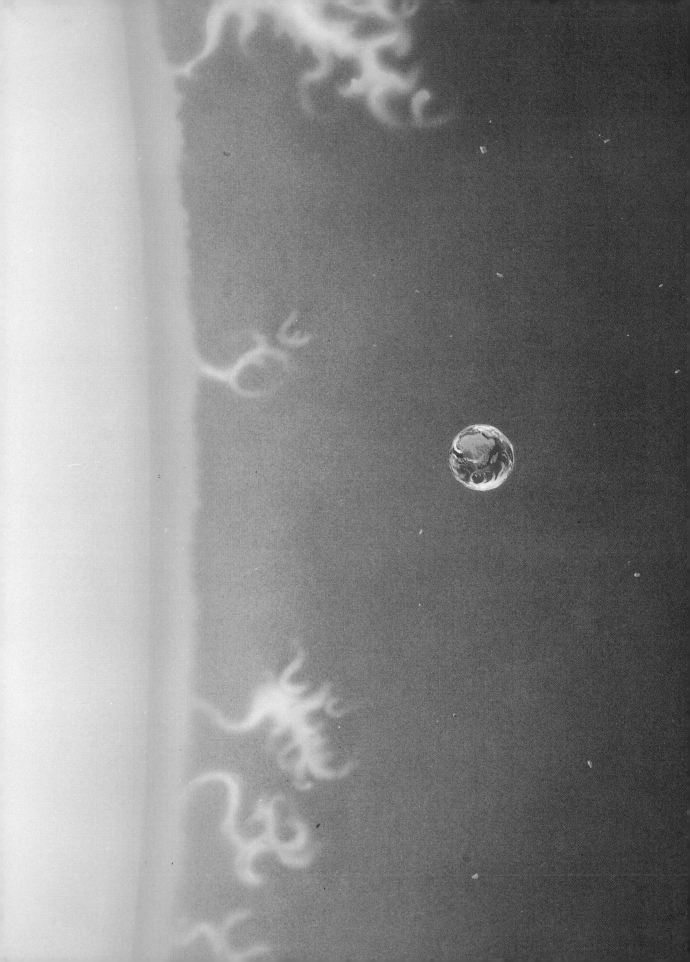

When stars are not stars

No matter how many shooting stars you spot, you will never see a real star streak by. Real stars are very different from shooting stars. They are huge, distant globes of hot gas that give off light and heat. Our Sun is a star. In this painting, you can see how huge it is compared with Earth.

Shooting stars are meteors – glowing bits of rock whizzing through the Earth's atmosphere. Stars glow for billions of years, but meteors flash for only a second. Stars cannot fall to Earth, but meteorites can.

The mysteries of meteors

We now know that shooting stars are not stars at all. They are meteors. But meteors themselves contain many mysteries. Through what strange regions have they passed on their far-flung journeys? What can they tell us about remote times and places, far from Earth? Our questions about meteors keep us wondering about our own world and about the fascinating mysteries of outer space.

22

Glossary

atmosphere: the gases that surround a planet, star or moon

comet: an object made of ice, rock, dust and gas which orbits the Sun. When it travels near the Sun, the comet develops a tail of gases which may be seen from Earth.

crater: a hole on a planet or moon gouged out by a meteorite

heavenly body: a star, planet, moon or other natural object that is found in space

iron: a silver or black metal that rusts in moist air; some meteorites contain iron

meteor: a piece of rock or dust travelling through the Earth's atmosphere

meteor shower: a period when a large number of meteors can be seen when the Earth is travelling through a dust cloud in space

meteorite: a meteor that hits the Earth

nickel: a hard, silvery metal used for making some coins; some meteorites contain nickel

star: a huge, hot, glowing globe of gases in outer space

Index